Thelwell's
Pony Panorama

thelwell's.
PONY
PANORAMA

GYMKHANA
THELWELL GOES WEST
PENELOPE

METHUEN

Published by Methuen 1999

3 5 7 9 10 8 6 4 2

First published in Great Britain in 1988 by Methuen London Ltd
Reissued in 1992

Reissued in 1999
by Methuen Publishing Limited
215 Vauxhall Bridge Road, London SW1V 1EJ

Thelwell's Pony Panorama copyright © 1988 Norman Thelwell
Thelwell's Penelope copyright © 1972 Norman Thelwell
Thelwell Goes West copyright © 1975 Norman Thelwell
Thelwell's Gymkhana copyright © 1979 Norman Thelwell

The right of Norman Thelwell to be identified as the author of
this work has been asserted by him in accordance with the
Copyright, Designs and Patents Act, 1988

Methuen Publishing Limited Reg. No. 3543167

A CIP catalogue record for this book is available from the British Library

ISBN 0 413 73850 7

Printed and bound in Great Britain by
Cox & Wyman Ltd, Reading, Berkshire

Papers used by Methuen Publishing Limited are natural, recyclable products
made from wood grown in sustainable forests. The manufacturing processes
conform to environmental regulations of the country of origin.

thelwell's
GYMKHANA

CONTENTS

Now you all know, of course,
  That the points of a horse
Are main features of every equine.
  But you'll find if you straddle
A horse with no saddle –
  They are all sticking up on his spine.

POINTS OF A HORSE

(WISE EQUESTRIANS ARE ADVISED TO STUDY THEM
FOR THEIR OWN SAFETY)

ASSEMBLY POINT

STARTING POINT

BOILING POINT

DANGER POINT

POINT OF DEPARTURE

POINT OF NO RETURN

BREAKING POINT

*   *   *

OH ANGELA'S TRAINING HER JUMPER
(WHEN DADDY COMES HOME HE'LL HAVE FITS)
SHE TRIED TO JUMP OVER THE BUMPER
AND KICKED HIS NEW BENTLEY TO BITS.

THE GAZEBO'S SMASHED IN THE HA HA
(THE GARDENER, I FEAR, MAY BE DEAD)
WHY DIDN'T I LISTEN TO GRANDPA
AND BUY HER A HAMSTER INSTEAD?

HOW TO TRAIN A JUMPER

PONIES OF ALMOST ANY TYPE CAN TURN OUT TO BE GOOD JUMPERS

POWERFUL HINDQUARTERS ARE A DISTINCT ADVANTAGE

AND SOUND FEET ESSENTIAL

THE MORE PONIES JUMP, THE MORE THEY SEEM TO LIKE IT

BUT MAKE SURE YOU KNOW HOW TO STOP THEM
BEFORE THEY GET OUT OF CONTROL

IF YOU BUY A READY MADE JUMPER HE MAY HAVE
DEVELOPED A STYLE WHICH YOU DO NOT PARTICULARLY LIKE

IT IS OFTEN BETTER TO BUY A COMPLETE NOVICE AND START
FROM SCRATCH

FIRST OF ALL YOU MUST GET YOUR PONY BALANCED

HE WILL NOT GET FAR OTHERWISE

THEN TEACH HIM HOW TO WALK CORRECTLY

INTRODUCE HIM TO EASY JUMPS UNTIL HE GAINS CONFIDENCE

HE WILL SOON TACKLE BIGGER OBSTACLES WITHOUT FEAR

PONIES ARE INCREDIBLY SENSITIVE TO ANY MOOD OR ATMOSPHERE

SO NEVER LOSE YOUR PATIENCE -

AND SOONER OR LATER ——

YOU'RE BOUND TO BE AMONG THE PRIZES

*　　　　　*　　　　　*

SO YOU'RE PICKING A PONY FOR LORNA?
(OH MUMMY, OH DADDY, THAT'S WIZ!)
BUT PLEASE DO NOT FORGET TO INFORM HER
THAT THE ADVERTS ARE SOMETIMES A SWIZ.

'HE HAS CARRIED A CHILD AT THE SHOW', DEAR,
MAY MEAN BY THE SEAT OF HER TREWS
AND IT'S FOOD (NOT THE FENCES) I KNOW, DEAR,
THAT HE'S 'NEVER BEEN KNOWN TO REFUSE.'

SO YOU'RE PICKING A PONY FOR LORNA,
TO WIN HER A ROSETTE OR CUP?
THEN MAKE SURE THERE'S A LEG AT EACH CORNER
AND DO NOT LET THEM SELL YOU A PUP.

PONIES FOR SALE

"THIS PONY HAS TAKEN MANY FIRST PRIZES."

" ... AN EXCELLENT LITTLE MOVER ... "

"... HAS OFTEN BEEN PLACED IN THE SHOW RING..."

" ... OWNER FORCED TO GIVE UP ... "

"... GENUINE REASON FOR SALE ..."

" . . . A WELL HANDLED PONY . . . "

"... ABLE TO TAKE BOTH WALLS AND TIMBER ..."

" . . . A GOOD ALL ROUNDER . . . "

" ...NOT YET BROKEN..."

"... HAS A SLIGHT BLEMISH ... "

"... AN IDEAL PONY FOR THE NERVOUS CHILD ... "

"...VERY QUIET IN THE STABLE..."

"...AT HOME IN TRAFFIC..."

" ...WELL KNOWN AT LOCAL SHOWS... "

"... A WALL-EYE PONY ... "

"... WELL ABLE TO COPE WITH ANY MEMBER OF THE FAMILY..."

*   *   *

'OH LET US RIDE,'THE LADIES CRIED,
  'WE'RE TIRED OF PLAYING HOCKEY.
WE CAN COMPETE AT ANY MEET
  WITH ANY OTHER JOCKEY.'

SO NOW THEY GALLOP WITH THE BOYS
  IN COLOURED SILKS AND BLOUSES
AND WHEN THEY FALL AT BECHER'S BROOK
  THEY SHOW WHO WEARS THE TROUSERS.

A DAY AT THE RACES
(A TINY TOTS' GUIDE TO THE TURF)

THE HOT FAVOURITE

GETTING ON THE BLOWER

FOUR TO ONE BAR

A NURSERY HANDICAP

SPRING DOUBLE

CALL OVER

BOTH WAYS

A RACING ACCUMULATOR

A GOOD STAYER

A BOOKIE'S PITCH

LAYING THE ODDS

ALSO RAN

PHOTO FINISH

*   *   *

THE OWNER OF A PONY MUST
  BE ONE A LITTLE HORSE CAN TRUST
    TO MUCK HIS STABLE OUT AT DAWN
      AND DUST HIS HAY AND WEIGH HIS CORN
AND SCRUB THE FLOOR WITH BRUSH AND HOSE
    UNTIL IT SHINES LIKE DADDY'S NOSE
  AND COMB HIS MANE AND CLEAN HIS TACK
  AND WATCH FOR WARBLES ON HIS BACK.
SO THINK OF WHAT EACH SEASON BRINGS
  AND CHECK HIS EARS FOR NASTY THINGS
AND GROOM HIS COAT AND DO NOT FAIL
  TO CLEAN HIS DOCK AND PULL HIS TAIL
  AND READ A BOOK OF HORSY HINTS
    AND FEEL HIS LEGS FOR SCARS AND SPLINTS
AND DRENCH HIM LEST HE SHOULD GET WORMS
AND SEARCH HIS DRINKING TROUGH FOR GERMS
AND KEEP ALERT FOR COUGHS AND SCOUR
  AND EXERCISE HIM FOR AN HOUR.
(DON'T GET HIM COLD OR MAKE HIM SWEAT
  OR YOU MAY HAVE TO CALL THE VET)
BEFORE YOU EAT YOUR BREAKFAST HADDOCK
MAKE SURE HE'S COMFY IN HIS PADDOCK.
  THEN OFF TO SCHOOL BEFORE YOU'RE LATE –
    AND PAT HIM AS YOU PASS THE GATE.

How to Keep Him Happy

NEVER CREEP UP SILENTLY BEHIND HIM
— OR YOU MAY GIVE HIM A FRIGHT

MAKE SURE YOU GIVE HIM ABOUT TWO HOURS OF STEADY EXERCISE
EVERY DAY

— BUT DO NOT KEEP HIM OUT UNTIL HE IS EXHAUSTED

GIVE HIM A COURSE OF SUPPLING EXERCISES –

AND MAKE SURE THAT HIS MUSCLES ARE WELL TONED UP

IF OUTDOOR EXERCISE IS NOT POSSIBLE —
GIVE HIS LEGS A GOOD HAND RUBBING

ENSURE THAT HIS FEET ARE KEPT PERFECTLY DRY AT ALL TIMES

EXAMINE HIS LEGS DAILY FOR SIGNS OF TROUBLE

BUT DO NOT BE TEMPTED TO OVER-BANDAGE HIM —
IT MAY OBSCURE HIS TRUE CONDITION

MAKE SURE HE CAN GET A DRINK OF WATER WHENEVER HE WANTS ONE

AND IF HE BOLTS HIS FOOD — TRY TO SPREAD IT OUT AS
WIDELY AS POSSIBLE

DO NOT ALLOW HIM TO EAT PLANTS WHICH MAY BE HARMFUL TO HIM

BUT PONIES LOVE NETTLES — SO WHY NOT GATHER
SOME FOR HIM FROM TIME TO TIME AND GIVE HIM A TREAT?

THE CHIEF DEFECT OF MANDY KING
    WAS BAD BEHAVIOUR IN THE RING.
SHE'D GALLOP IN BEFORE THE BELL,
    DO OTHER NAUGHTY THINGS AS WELL
LIKE PUSHING SUSAN TO THE GROUND
    BECAUSE SHE'D HAD A FAULTLESS ROUND
AND GIVING PEOPLE NASTY LOOKS
    AND LETTING BOUNCER KICK LORD SNOOKS.
WHEN ASKED TO LEAVE SHE WOULD NOT BUDGE
    BUT MADE RUDE FACES AT THE JUDGE

- SO AS I'M SURE YOU WILL SURMISE,
    THEY ONLY GAVE HER SECOND PRIZE

HOW TO BEHAVE IN THE SHOW RING

ALWAYS ENTER THE ARENA WITH CONFIDENCE —
NERVOUSNESS MAY COMMUNICATE ITSELF TO YOUR PONY

DO NOT ALLOW HIM TO BE PUT OFF BY SPECTATORS —

OR CROWDED OUT BY OTHER COMPETITORS

REMEMBER TO SALUTE THE JUDGE

AND KEEP YOUR SHOW SIMPLE — YOU ARE SHOWING OFF
YOUR PONY , NOT YOURSELF

AND **NEVER** DISPUTE HIS DECISION

IF YOU SHOULD WIN, DO NOT GET HYSTERICAL

EXCESSIVE PRAISE OF YOUR PONY MAY SUGGEST THAT
YOU ARE NOT USED TO SUCCESS

IF YOU ARE DUE FOR A PRIZE, DO NOT BE BLASÉ ABOUT
RECEIVING IT

— AND MOST IMPORTANT OF ALL —

KEEP IN YOUR CORRECT ORDER WHEN RIDING IN THE LAP OF HONOUR

✳   ✳   ✳

SUE HAD A LITTLE PONY, PETE,
  WHO GALLOPED ROUND ON PEOPLE'S FEET
AND THREW HER OFF AND WOULD NOT HALT,
  WHICH WAS ENTIRELY SUSAN'S FAULT.
EQUESTRIANS (AND HORSEMEN TOO)
  GAVE GOOD ADVICE BUT SADLY, SUE
REFUSED TO DO WHAT SHE WAS TOLD
  SO FAILED TO WIN OLYMPIC GOLD.

IF SHE HAD ONLY READ THESE TIPS
  SHE MIGHT HAVE WON SOME CHAMPIONSHIPS.

RULES FOR RIDERS

PONIES ARE GREGARIOUS — SO TRY TO GIVE HIM
AS MUCH COMPANIONSHIP AS POSSIBLE

DO NOT USE FORCE TO GET YOUR OWN WAY
— HE IS STRONGER THAN YOU ARE —

SO GET HIM TO DO WHAT YOU WANT BY GENTLE PERSUASION

NEVER TRY TO THROW HIM UNLESS YOU ARE AN EXPERT

TEACH HIM TO STAND QUIETLY WHATEVER
YOU MAY BE DOING IN THE SADDLE

IF HE MAKES A MISTAKE —

REMEMBER IT IS YOUR FAULT — NOT HIS

BUT IF HE MISBEHAVES YOU MUST TAKE ACTION IMMEDIATELY

IF YOU GO HUNTING —

DO NOT FORGET TO LET THE MASTER KNOW YOU ARE THERE

AND SHOUT 'HOLLOA AWAY' ONLY WHEN
YOU ARE QUITE SURE THE FOX HAS GONE

DO NOT FORGET TO CONTRIBUTE TO THE DAMAGE FUND

AND ALWAYS GIVE A CHEERY 'GOOD NIGHT' TO
ANYONE YOU MAY MEET ON THE WAY HOME

✳   ✳   ✳

DADDY, THEY SAY, HAD A TERRIBLE DAY.
HE'S BEEN SLAVING AWAY SINCE DAWN
HE'S TAKEN A POWDER AND HIT THE HAY
SO DON'T RIDE OVER HIS LAWN.

MUMMY'S IN BED WITH A SPLITTING HEAD
THERE'S DINNER ALL OVER THE WALL
THE COOKER BLEW UP AND THE BUDGIE'S DEAD
SO DON'T RIDE INTO THE HALL.

GRANDMOTHER'S HIP IS GIVING HER GYP
AND GRANDFATHER'S RACKED WITH PAIN
— SO **PLEASE** DON'T GALLOP HIM UP THE STAIRS
— OR SOMEBODY MIGHT COMPLAIN.

.thelwell.
GOES WEST

CONTENTS

BULL FINCH

RIDING HABIT

VIEW HALLOO

SADDLE SORE

WHIPPERS IN

HORSE TRAILER

HAY BAG

FOLLOWERS

THRUSTERS

THE ENGLISH RIDER

LITTLE BIG HORN

VIGILANTES

PALE FACE

COW HAND

DEAD WOOD

RAW HIDE

RATTLERS

RUSTLERS

FRONTIER

CHUCK WAGGON

BRAND X

THE WESTERN HORSEMAN

WESTERN RIDING

EFORE TAKING UP WESTERN RIDING – IT IS IMPORTANT TO STUDY THE COWBOY SEAT

IN THE WEST, RIDERS FIND IT MORE COMFORTABLE TO SIT AS LOW AS POSSIBLE
IN THE SADDLE —

AND TO KEEP ONE HAND FREE OF THE REINS AT ALL TIMES

ASK THEM TO SHOW YOU THEIR HANDS, WHEN YOU GET A CHANCE AND —

NOTICE THE RELAXED POSITION ADOPTED BY MOST COWBOYS WHEN RIDING THE RANGE

— OR WHEN THEY HIT TOWN

THE EASTERN RIDER LIKES TO BUMP UP AND DOWN IN THE SADDLE

THIS IS ALL VERY WELL OVER SHORT DISTANCES

BUT REMEMBER —

THE COW-HAND MAY BE ON THE TRAIL FOR WEEKS AT A TIME

WHEN COMMUNICATING HIS WISHES TO HIS HORSE, THE COWBOY
DOES SO VIA THE ANIMAL'S NECK

SOME ENGLISH METHODS ARE NOT CONSIDERED GOOD PRACTICE

WHEN OUT ON THE RANGE —

YOUR SURVIVAL MAY WELL DEPEND UPON YOUR PONY'S NATURAL COURAGE —

AND SUREFOOTEDNESS

SO TREAT HIM LIKE A FRIEND

WHAT TO WEAR

THE RIDERS OF THE WEST ARE EASY-GOING, OUTDOOR
GUYS AND GALS AND LOVE TO TRAVEL LIGHT —

THEY PRIDE THEMSELVES ON THEIR SIMPLE AND PRACTICAL FORM OF DRESS

AND ARE INCLINED TO GREET FANCY CLOTHES WITH AMUSEMENT

THE SADDLE IS HEAVIER AND MORE COMPLICATED THAN YOU MAY HAVE BEEN USED TO —

SO MAKE SURE YOU KNOW HOW TO PUT IT ON CORRECTLY

WHEN DONE BY AN EXPERT, IT ALL LOOKS VERY SIMPLE

DON'T FORGET TO TIGHTEN UP THE CINCHES

WESTERN HORSES

THE MUSTANG

KNOWN THE WORLD OVER FOR HIS UNIQUE CONTRIBUTION TO
THE MOTION PICTURE INDUSTRY, THIS LOVABLE HORSE HAS
APPEARED IN MORE FILMS THAN BILLY-THE-KID

THE QUARTER HORSE

HAS GREAT CATTLE SENSE AND IS ABLE TO GET OFF THE
MARK WITH ASTONISHING SPEED

THE BRONCO
HIS NAME COMES FROM THE SPANISH WORD MEANING ROUGH & RUDE

THE PINTO
OR PAINTED HORSE

NATURAL CAMOUFLAGE GAVE THIS ANIMAL A GREAT ADVANTAGE IN BATTLE
HE WAS MUCH FAVOURED BY THE INDIANS WHEN ON THE WAR·PATH —

SO WAS THE **APALOOSA** OR SPOTTED HORSE

THE AMERICAN SADDLE HORSE

FAMOUS FOR HIS ABILITY TO EXECUTE AN ASTONISHING VARIETY OF SPECTACULAR GAITS

THE MORGAN HORSE

THIS STRIKING LITTLE ANIMAL HAS LEFT HIS IMPRINT
ON ALMOST EVERY OTHER AMERICAN BREED

THE PALOMINO

KNOWN AS THE GOLDEN HORSE OF THE WEST, THIS HANDSOME CREATURE
IS POPULAR WITH ALL THOSE WHO APPRECIATE NATURAL BEAUTY

QUICK ON THE DRAWL

TO UNDERSTAND THE COWBOY'S WAY OF LIFE IT IS ADVISABLE TO KNOW THE MEANING OF CERTAIN WORDS AND PHRASES MUCH USED BY THE EXPERTS

HERE ARE A FEW :-

TENDER FOOT (OR HOP-A-LONG)

SIDE KICKS

THE LONE STRANGER

A SOD BUSTER OR —

GETTING YOURSELF A LITTLE SPREAD

SPEAKING WITH FORKED TONGUE

HIGH NOON

GETTING THE DROP ON A GUY

LOOKING DOWN THE BARREL OF A COLT

GET A LONG LITTLE DOGIE

HOW TO UNDERSTAND YOUR HORSE

HORSES CANNOT TALK . IT IS USEFUL, THEREFORE, TO HAVE
SOME IDEA OF WHAT THEY MAY BE THINKING

IMPORTANT CLUES TO YOUR PONY'S THOUGHTS MAY BE GLEANED
BY CLOSE OBSERVATION OF HIS EARS

FOR EXAMPLE : —

" I INTEND TO SHOOT OFF TO THE LEFT "

" YOU HAVE SHOT OFF TO THE RIGHT "

143

" THERE'S A NASTY WIND BLOWING UP "

" MAKE FOR COVER — IT'S A TWISTER "

"I AM GOING TO GALLOP UNDER THIS LOW TREE BRANCH"

" WHAT A DREADFUL NAME TO CALL A PONY "

" YOU WANT TO CHASE COWS — YOU CHASE COWS "

" YOU'LL NEVER GET ME UP IN ONE OF THOSE THINGS"

NOTICE HIS GENERAL DEMEANOUR

YOU WILL SOON LEARN WHAT HE IS TRYING TO SAY :-

" OOH! OOH! I'VE TRODDEN ON YOUR GUITAR "

" IT SOUNDED LIKE A RATTLE-SNAKE TO ME "

" IT'S FREEZING OUT THERE ON THE PRAIRIE "

" ALL THIS RIDING OFF INTO THE SUNSET IS RUINING MY EYES "

ON THE TRAIL

BEFORE SADDLING UP - MAKE SURE YOUR HORSE IS
HEALTHY, ALERT AND READY TO GO —

HE SHOULD BE TRAINED TO STEP OVER FALLEN TIMBER WITHOUT HESITATION

AND BE PREPARED TO CARRY EXTRA LOADS WHEN CALLED UPON TO DO SO

HE MUST NOT SPOOK
AT HARMLESS OBJECTS

156

OR BLUNDER HEADLONG INTO DANGEROUS ONES

DO NOT GET ANXIOUS ON DIFFICULT TERRAIN
   - YOU MAY COMMUNICATE YOUR FEELINGS TO YOUR HORSE

AND <u>DON'T</u> LEAN OVER IN THE SADDLE WHEN TIRED

YOU MAY UPSET HIS BALANCE

ALWAYS DISMOUNT ON THE UPHILL
SIDE OF YOUR PONY

AND IF YOU START AN AVALANCHE - SHOUT A WARNING TO RIDERS BELOW

BE PREPARED TO TRUST HIS NATURAL INSTINCTS AND ABILITIES WHEN CROSSING
NARROW BRIDGES

AND DO NOT ALLOW HIM INTO WATER IF HE IS HOT

IN VERY HOT CONDITIONS - ALLOW HIM TO TAKE ADVANTAGE OF ANY
AVAILABLE SHADE

AND RAISE HIS SADDLE FROM TIME TO TIME TO LET THE AIR CIRCULATE

IT IS BAD MANNERS TO RIDE TOO CLOSE TO THE HORSE IN FRONT

OR TO ATTEMPT TO OVERTAKE ON A NARROW TRAIL

AND MOST IMPORTANT OF ALL —

NEVER RIDE OVER PRIVATE PROPERTY WITHOUT FIRST OBTAINING
THE OWNER'S CONSENT

HOW TO MANAGE A MEAN HORSE

REFUSING TO BE CAUGHT

THIS CAN BE VERY TRYING. DECOY HIM TO SOME CONVENIENT SPOT AND BE READY
TO SLIP A ROPE OVER HIS HEAD WITHOUT AROUSING HIS SUSPICION

MOVING OFF WHEN ABOUT TO BE MOUNTED

AN EXASPERATING HABIT. TRY THE OLD INDIAN TRICK OF LEADING HIM INTO A BOG AND MOUNTING UP WHILST HIS MOVEMENT IS RESTRICTED

BLANKET TEARING

HE IS PROBABLY BORED — TRY SINGING A DIFFERENT SONG

VIOLENT PULLING ON THE REINS

THIS CAN UNSEAT A RIDER -

HAVE A LOOK AT HIS MOUTH - HE MAY HAVE SORE TEETH

CRIB BITING

THE ANIMAL SHOULD BE ISOLATED - THE HABIT IS CATCHING

WIND SUCKING

GET RID OF THE HORSE - THE RESULTS CAN BE ALARMING

BITING

CAN OFTEN BE CURED - STOP CARRYING SUGAR LUMPS IN YOUR
BACK POCKET

SUDDEN REARING

THE ANSWER HERE IS TO SLIP OUT OF THE SADDLE WHENEVER HE DOES IT

ROLLING

THIS IS NATURAL TO A HORSE AND ONE OF HIS CHIEF JOYS

DO NOT LET IT DEPRESS YOU

BOLTING

TRY JERKING HIS HEAD VIOLENTLY BACKWARDS AND FORWARDS
BY PULLING ON THE REINS - THE IDEA HERE IS THAT IT
WILL TEND TO CONFUSE HIM

KICKING

MAY WELL BE CAUSED BY NERVOUSNESS - TRY TO COMFORT AND REASSURE HIM

SAVAGING

A FRIGHTENING SIGHT - DROP EVERYTHING - RUN LIKE A JACK RABBIT

HOW TO CROSS WATER

DO NOT TRY TO FORCE HIM INTO THE WATER AGAINST HIS WILL

DEMONSTRATE TO HIM THAT THE WATER IS HARMLESS

HE WILL GO IN WHEN HE IS READY

DO NOT DISMOUNT AND LEAD HIM FROM IN FRONT

HE IS LIKELY TO CLIMB ON TO ANYTHING THAT LOOKS SOLID

MAKE SURE YOU KNOW HOW TO
ADMINISTER THE KISS OF LIFE —

YOU NEVER KNOW WHO MAY NEED IT

RODEO DOUGH

A GREAT DEAL OF MONEY GOES INTO THE RODEO RING THESE DAYS
SO IT IS AS WELL TO STUDY SOME OF THE RULES

188

AND TO PERFORM A PATTERN OF MOVEMENT EXACTLY AS
SPECIFIED BY THE JUDGES

SOME RIDERS CHOOSE TO
DEMONSTRATE THEIR SKILL
IN THE SADDLE

SOME PERFORM BAREBACK

OTHERS APPEAR TO BE HAPPIER ON A BULL

EACH RIDER MUST STAY
ABOARD FOR A SPECIFIED
NUMBER OF SECONDS

AND MUST RAKE THE SHOULDERS
OF HIS MOUNT CONTINUOUSLY
WITH HIS HEELS

ON NO ACCOUNT MUST HE TOUCH HIS HORSE WITH HIS HANDS

A MILD MANNERED ANIMAL MAY COST HIM VALUABLE POINTS —

BUT EXTRA MARKS MAY BE AWARDED FOR STYLE

IN CASE OF DOUBT —

THE COMPETITOR MAY BE ASKED TO REPEAT HIS PERFORMANCE

WESTERN QUIZ

Q.   WHY IS THIS COWBOY SHOOTING UP THE TOWN ?

A.   BECAUSE HIS HORSE STOPPED SUDDENLY ON MAIN STREET

Q. IS THIS GUY A BRONCO BUSTER?

A. NO, BUT HE SOON WILL BE IF HE GOES ON FEEDING CORN AT THAT RATE

Q. STUDY THIS PICTURE. HOW CAN YOU TELL THAT THIS IS A BAD MAN?

A. HE HAS NEGLECTED TO CHECK HIS HORSE'S FEET FOR ROCKS

Q. WHAT IS MEANT BY THE EXPRESSION 'WINDY DRAWS'?

A. IT IS A TERM OF CONTEMPT FOR NERVOUS COWBOYS

Q. THIS PONY HAS FOUR WEAK POINTS – WHAT ARE THEY ?

A. HIS LEGS

Q.   WHY IS THIS CONSIDERED BAD RIDING OUT WEST?

A.   THE HEAD SHOULD BE UP AND THE HEELS DOWN

Q. IS THIS COWPOKE BEING CHASED BY A POSSE ?

A. NO. THE CORRECT NAME IS COUGAR OR MOUNTAIN LION

Q. WHY IS THIS RIDER LOOKING UNCOMFORTABLE ?

A. HIS JEANS ARE TOO TIGHT

Q.   WOULD YOU CALL THIS GUY A SADDLE TRAMP ?

A.   IF IT WAS YOUR SADDLE YOU WOULD

Q WHAT IS WRONG WITH THIS PICTURE ?

A. THE RIDER HAS GOT THE WRONG FOOT IN THE STIRRUP

Q. WHAT IMPORTANT RULE DID THIS RIDER NEGLECT?

A. SHE DID NOT CHECK THE BRAND BEFORE BUYING HER PONY.

AND FINALLY — WHAT IS THE MOST IMPORTANT RULE TO REMEMBER?

THAT'S RIGHT! <u>NEVER</u> HOLD ONTO THE REINS WITH BOTH HANDS

Penelope

by

thelwell.

This book is based on a series
which appeared in the Sunday Express

I DON'T THINK MUCH OF HIS SEAT.

" I'LL BE GLAD WHEN SHE GETS INTERESTED IN BOYS. "

229

" COME ALONG GIRLS . PLAY TIME'S OVER "

"WHAT A SHAME! THERE GOES HER EGG AND SPOON."

253

258

" SHE'S NOT MAKING VERY RAPID PROGRESS, I'M AFRAID "

" SHE LOVES THAT PONY – NEVER OUT OF THE SADDLE "

I'M WORRIED ABOUT KIPPER, FIONA. HE'S GOT A TOUCH OF INSOMNIA!

I'M SURE I'M RIGHT BUT I'D APPRECIATE A SECOND OPINION

THERE! DID YOU SEE THAT EYELID FLICKER?

287

290

" HURRY UP! I'M ON HORSEBACK. "